PUFFIN BOOKS

D0726563

CHECK OUT CHESS

With stars like the world champion Gary Kasparov from the
Soviet Union and Britain's own Nigel Short, chess is reaching
new heights of popularity. Now Bob Wade, one of the
best-known names in British chess, and Ted Nottingham, a
teacher highly experienced in introducing children to this
enduring game, have written a new and original first book for
all would-be chess stars.

From setting out the pieces on the board to such sophisti-
cated techniques as the skewer and discovered attack, the
authors lead the beginner step by step through the basic
principles. There are many fun exercises and simple games
specially designed to develop the sound knowledge and skills
so necessary to become a successful player.

Entertaining stories from chess's colourful past and moves
from the games of champions add to make this a unique and
valuable introduction to the 'game of kings'.

Ted Nottingham is a primary school teacher in Lincoln-
shire and has been editor of the English Primary Schools
Chess Magazine 'Move'. He also devised the Lincolnshire
Method, an internationally acclaimed method of teaching the
game. Bob Wade was born in New Zealand but has long been
involved in the organization of chess in Britain and has
written and edited many specialist books on the game. He is
England's Chief Trainer. In 1986 he was referee to the World
Championship in Leningrad between Gary Kasparov and
Anatoly Karpov, and in 1988 referee to Nigel Short and Jon
Spielmann in their World Championship quarter-final
match.

CHECK OUT CHESS

Bob Wade and Ted Nottingham
Illustrated by Raymond Turvey

PUFFIN BOOKS

PUFFIN BOOKS

Published by the Penguin Group
27 Wrights Lane, London w8 5tz, England
Viking Penguin Inc., 40 West 23rd Street, New York, New York 10010, USA
Penguin Books Australia Ltd, Ringwood, Victoria, Australia
Penguin Books Canada Ltd, 2801 John Street, Markham, Ontario, Canada l3r 1b4
Penguin Books (NZ) Ltd, 182–190 Wairau Road, Auckland 10, New Zealand

Penguin Books Ltd, Registered Offices: Harmondsworth, Middlesex, England

Published in Puffin Books 1989
10 9 8 7 6 5 4 3 2 1

Diagrams by Square One

Made and printed in Great Britain by
Cox and Wyman Ltd, Reading, Berks
Filmset in Linotron Imprint by
Rowland Phototypesetting Ltd, Bury St Edmunds, Suffolk

Acknowledgements

The authors would like to thank:

Al Lawrence, director of the US Chess Federation for his stories 'The Game of Kings' and 'Making a Map'.
The late Mrs Phyllis Woodall of Boston for her poem 'The Book is Ended'.
Dorothy Cox for typing, Hilary Thomas for layout, and Mrs Coby Fairbanks for proof-reading.
Maurice Lyon for being a thorough and decisive editor.
'How a Chess Game Stopped a Battle: A True Story' is based on Tom Driberg's report in *Reynolds News* in 1947.
'The Merchant and the Arab' is based on a story from *Sakmat* by M. Jokai.

CONTENTS

INTRODUCTION

HOW A CHESS GAME STOPPED A BATTLE:
A TRUE STORY

It was summer 1944. Just as the Western Allies were pouring through France on their way to Germany, so on the Eastern front the Soviet Red Army was making a big push against the German divisions massed there. A fourteen-year-old boy sat below ground with a few others in an air-raid cellar in Budapest, the capital city of Hungary. Hand-to-hand fighting raged in the city outside as the Germans were being pushed back by Soviet soldiers. The young Hungarian sat playing chess with a German soldier, safe for a while from the noise and fighting outside. Suddenly other Germans burst in and ordered their fellow German out. Red Army soldiers were in the street! The Germans had to run immediately. A few minutes later, a Soviet soldier burst in waving his sub-machine gun at everybody in the cellar. One woman screamed. Then the soldier saw the chess game and the young Hungarian boy sitting before it. Only a young man himself, he lowered his gun. He sat down on the other side of the board and won the game that the German – his enemy – had started. After the war, the young Hungarian said that those two soldiers, the German and the Soviet, were two of the nicest people he had ever met!

The moral of this story is clear. Chess is an international game, crossing all boundaries, even those of war. Even 'enemies' who cannot speak each other's language can play together. After you have read this book, you will be able to play chess with anybody, young or old, of any nationality.

THE GAME OF KINGS

Chess is exciting. It is a 'war' game. There is a white army fighting against a black army. Both sides start out equal. Both play to win! Pawns, rooks, bishops, knights and even queens 'fall' in the chess battle. But neither of the two players – the 'generals' who move the chess pieces – is ever hurt, no matter how hard the fight!

There is a legend that centuries ago in India squabbles were settled not by a terrible war but by a game of chess.

When two rulers disagreed, they would not send their soldiers out to hurt and kill one another with swords and spears and arrows. Instead, the kings themselves would fight. But they would fight with their brains, not their muscles. They would play a game of chess. The winner of the chess game would get his way. The argument was settled and no one was hurt. Later chess spread to the courts of Europe, becoming truly the game of kings.

Chess was first played in India about 1400 years ago. However, we owe the spread of the game to the Arabs of the eighth and ninth centuries A.D., who also loved the game very much. The Arabs produced some great players. The first books and manuscripts on chess positions date from this time. Chess is now played all over the world and we are able to read and play through games from around the globe.

This book will introduce you to the 'game of kings'.

ENJOY CHESS

The one aim in chess is to give checkmate to, or to capture, the opponent's king. To enjoy chess you will need to know how your pieces can attack and capture and you will need to move your pieces with effect – with punch!

To develop your skills, you must learn

- to look and instantly to see all the squares to which a moved piece can go
- to see and to build up checkmating positions, even in the middle of many other pieces
- to use tactics like forks, pins and ambushes to exploit the strengths of your side and the weaknesses of the opponent's
- to battle to make your pieces more and more active and to keep your opponent's quiet and not working
- after *every* move, to seek an answer to the question 'What is my opponent trying to do?', to see how you can be attacked or your plans upset before you decide between continuing your plan, attacking, counter-attacking, defending or finding a new plan
- to use basic finishing skills, like the ending with king and queen against lone king

These skills can be achieved by playing through and studying the great games and positions of past and present champions. Many of the games in this book are specially designed to make you instantly and totally familiar with the action of each chessman. In chess, the winner is nearly always the player who has the most active pieces and who uses them all as a team.

You need constant practice and good opponents to make you excel at chess. So bring out your chessboard and pieces, set up the positions, and find a worthy friend to test the games in this, your first, training manual.

MAPPING THE CHESSBOARD

Naming the squares

Chess players all over the world use the same simple language to name the squares of the chessboard. It's called *algebraic notation*, a fancy name for an easy language. We map the chessboard by using just the first eight letters of the alphabet: a, b, c, d, e, f, g, h. We also use the numbers 1 through to 8. We use these letters and numbers to name the columns and rows of squares on the chessboard.

Files

Beginning from White's left-hand side, we label the up-and-down columns of squares a through to h. These up-and-down columns of squares which stretch between the players are called *files*. There are eight files.

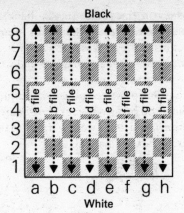

Ranks

We number the left-to-right rows 1 through to 8, starting with White's side of the board. These left-to-right rows are called *ranks*.

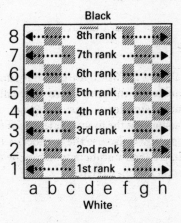

Each square on the chessboard has an address, much like your own home has an address. A square's address is the letter and number of the *file* and *rank* that cross through it, like streets.

The right-hand-corner square nearest White is where the h-file and the 1st rank meet. This square is called h1.

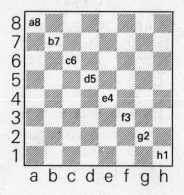

Black's right-hand corner is where the a-file and the 8th rank cross. It's called a8.

In the diagram below, what square have we put a question mark in?

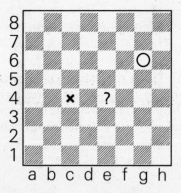

Run your finger up or down from the square to find its file address. Then put your finger back on the square and move it to the left or right to find its rank address. Put the file and rank together to give the square's complete address: e4.

What square is the cross in?
How about the circle?
If you said the cross was in c4, and the circle was in g6, you
were right!

Easy, isn't it? This is the language used by chess players all
over the world. With it, you can recreate great games and
learn from them. You can also write down your own games!
Then you can play over the moves again and improve on
them.

Position of the board

Notice the squares are dark and light coloured.

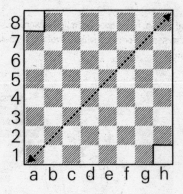

The board is placed so that each player has a white square in their bottom right-hand corner.

Notice that a black square is in the nearest left-hand corner, and a diagonal row of black squares runs from a1 to h8, or h8 to a1.

1. HOW THE CHESSMEN MOVE

'Tenuous king, slant bishop, bitter queen, straightforward castle and the crafty pawn—over the checkered black and white terrain they seek out and enjoin their armed campaign.'

J. L. Borges, *Chess*
(translated by A. Reid)

THE KING ♔

The king is your most important piece, the leader of your army. Let it be captured and you have lost the game.

The king can move one square at a time in any direction. That means it can be moved one square forwards or backwards or sideways or one square along a diagonal.

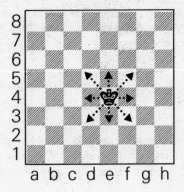

In this position, the king is on the square e4. It could be moved to d4 or f5 or e3, for example. Or it could be played to d5 or e5 or f4 or f3 or d3.

How many different ways can the king get from e1 to e4 in three moves? We thought there were seven. Do you agree?

Try from e1 to e5 in four moves. Did you find nineteen?

What's the least number of moves for the king to travel from e1 to a8? The least number is seven.

The king can capture an opponent's pieces if they occupy a square to which the king can move. In order to capture, simply move the king to the square occupied by the opponent's piece and remove that piece from the board.

Bishops used to be powerful advisers to the kings.

Each player starts with two bishops. The bishops can move any number of squares diagonally; they cannot jump over other pieces.

Look at the diagram below. The whole chessboard has sixty-four squares. Not counting the squares they are standing on, the two bishops can move to, and thus control or attack, twenty-six squares. They can be a powerful team.

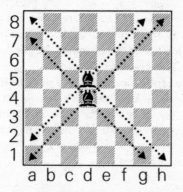

The bishop captures by being placed on the square occupied by the opponent's piece and then removing that piece from the board.

If the white pawns remain fixed, how many moves would it take the bishop to capture them all? It should take six moves. Remember you can only capture one piece at a time.

The bishop travels via f4, d6, e7, h4, f2 to b6.

How many squares can the bishop go to in this diagram?

Remember: he cannot jump on to or over his own pieces.
Thirteen squares? Wrong.
Five squares? Wrong.
Six squares? Right!

Together the two bishops could go to every square on the board. For this reason, good players may go to some trouble to prevent either being captured.

THE ROOK ♜

Rook is the proper chess name for the piece that looks like a castle, even though some people outside chess circles call it a castle.

Each player starts with two rooks. The rooks can move any number of squares forwards or backwards along the files or sideways along the ranks. But – like the bishop – the rook can only move in one direction at a time, and usually it cannot jump over other pieces.

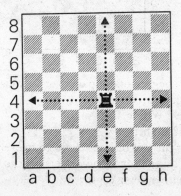

In the previous diagram the rook can be moved to e8, to a4, to e1, to h4, or to any square between.

Below, capture all the black pieces with the white rook in nine moves! When you capture, take off the black piece and put the white rook in its place. Remember: just nine moves.

Did you take first on d1? Wrong.

Did you take the c4, c7, g7, g3, d3, d1, f1, f5, f6 route? Right!

THE QUEEN ♛

The queen is the starship of the chessboard, able to accelerate at will in any direction. The queen can move vertically, horizontally and diagonally, but only in one direction each time. She cannot jump.

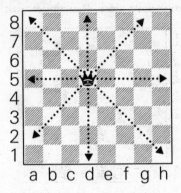

She can be played from d5 to a8, to d8, to g8, to a5, to h5, to a2, to d1, to h1, or to any square between.

The queen was not always so powerful. In the Middle Ages, she could only move two squares on any move. In the early 1490s, about the same time that Columbus was busy discovering America, the Spaniards and Italians introduced the new go-everywhere rule for the queen. This new queen, 'the mad queen', could even finish off a game in only two moves.

Can you take all five black pieces with the white queen in five moves? The black pieces stand still.

Try f3, g3, c7, . . . There are also three other routes to achieve this.

THE KNIGHT

The knight's move is **L**-shaped. He's played two squares along the file or rank and then one to the right or left, and he jumps over anything in his path.

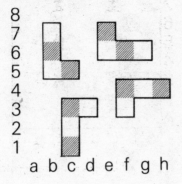

From a light square, he goes to a dark square. Any enemy piece foolish enough to land on any of the squares marked with a cross below is liable to fall victim to the knight's deadly leap. And, if he is on a dark square, he jumps in **L**-shaped fashion to the light squares.

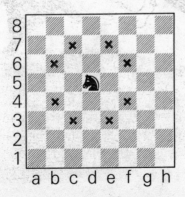

Knight on L-Plates

How many moves does the white knight need to capture the black pawn from

1. g5?
2. d7?
3. e7?
4. c7?
5. d8?

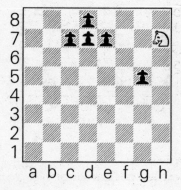

Answers:

1. 1 direct.
2. 2 via f6 or f8.
3. 3 via f6 and g8, f6 and d5, or f8 and g6.
4. 3 via f8 and e6 or f6 and e8.
5. 3 via f8 and e6, g5 and e6, or g5 and f7.

Knight's Jog

How many moves does it take a knight to go from g1 to g8?

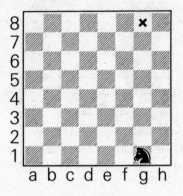

Did you do it in five?
How many moves does it take a knight to go from h1 to a8?

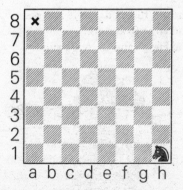

Did you manage it in six?

THE PAWN

There are eight pawns on each side to start with. These pawns are limited and seem weak. They are used to open doors and lines. They are given away to help big pieces to attack. But at the end of the file there's a prize for each of them: they can be promoted to a queen; or you can choose to make them any other piece except a king.

How Pawns Move

The Arabs of the eighth century moved the pawn only one square on the first move. Moderns thought this boring! The two armies took a long time to meet. Now each pawn can be moved either one or two squares forwards on its first move. After that, the pawn can only move one square forwards at a time.

How Pawns Capture

To capture, the pawn moves one square *diagonally* forwards.
It cannot take a piece on the square directly in front of it. The
white pawn in the diagram can capture the opponent's knight
or rook on its next move.

Below, the pawns' ways are blocked: there are pieces straight
ahead of them. None of the pawns can advance any further.

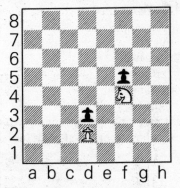

They have to wait until the obstructions are moved or until
something comes along which they can capture diagonally.

MOVING AND CAPTURING

At the beginning of the game, the player who has the white
pieces moves first. This is a tradition many centuries old.
Then Black replies, and thereafter each player makes one
move in turn.

Capturing, or taking, your opponent's pieces is one of the most important things to get right in the game of chess. Quite often, your decision to take a piece will be determined by the swap value of the pieces you gain and lose in the exchange.

Swap Value of the Pieces

PAWN = 1 pawn
KNIGHT = 3 pawns
BISHOP = 3 pawns
ROOK = 5 pawns
QUEEN = 9 pawns

But, you might say, I haven't got nine pawns. The queen's value is made up of one rook, one knight (or bishop) and one pawn: 5 + 3 + 1 = 9.

Would you take the rook with the white queen? Is it a good idea? The answer is no! If you take the rook with your queen, then your opponent can take your queen with the pawn. A rook is worth five points; a queen, nine. So, you win five, but lose nine: a bad bargain!

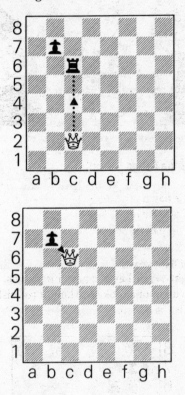

WRITE YOUR MOVES

Chess players use a kind of shorthand to write down each move of a game. Thus, a game can be permanently recorded. To show you how it works, this is how the above exchange is written.

White plays the queen from c2 to c6 and takes the rook. This is written as

$$Qc2 \times c6$$

where

Q stands for queen
c2 is the departure square
× stands for 'takes'
c6 is the square of arrival, from which the black rook is removed and replaced by the white queen.

If the white queen had moved on to an empty square without capturing, we would have written Qc2–c6, where '–' means 'moves to'.

We will assume that it's White's 32nd move, and Black's 32nd move in reply is, unkindly, pawn takes queen. We write both moves as

32 Qc2 × c6   b7 × c6

We do not need to write P for pawn as this will have been clear from the previous moves.

TOUCH AND MOVE RULE

In chess, there is a touch and move rule. This is partly to stop disputes, but it is also a very useful discipline to make you really think out and be sure of your move. The strict rule is that, if you touch a piece, you must move it, and, if you touch an enemy piece, you must take it if the rules allow. If a piece does need straightening, we say '*j'adoube*' or '*I adjust*' *first*.

Did You Know?

There was a murder committed over the touch and move rule. On St Michael's Day in the year 1027 at the Danish capital of Roskilde, King Canute the Great sat down with his Earl Ulf at a game of chess. In the course of the game, Canute blundered. Ulf would not let him take his piece back, and was so furious with the king for asking that he knocked the board over. Next morning, the king's men did Ulf to death. Today, we stick strictly to the touch and move rule. We don't want any more incidents like that!

2. ATTACKING AND DEFENDING

'Chess is life.'

Bobby Fischer, World Champion 1972–1975

In this chapter, we discuss basic tactics for attack and defence. We show you how to attack your opponent's king and put it under threat of capture – to put it in check – and we show you how to defend yourself in such situations. Finally, we show you how the game is won, by forcing the opponent's king into such a position that he cannot avoid capture – checkmate!

TURN DEFENCE INTO ATTACK

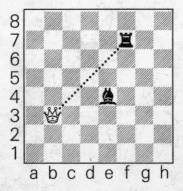

In this position, the queen attacks the black rook. The rook can move out of the way. Let's look for a safe square.

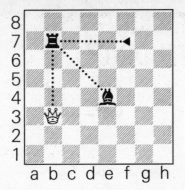

The rook has moved to a square where, not only is it defended by the bishop, but from where it attacks the queen. It would be a bad idea for White to take the rook with the queen, as Black's bishop could then capture the queen. White's loss would then be equal to four pawns.

CHECK

If the king is in a position where it can be captured, it is said to be in check.

Black king in check to white rook.

Black king in check to white bishop.

White king in check to black knight.

White king in check to black queen.

If your king is in check, then you must save it on your next move. It is against the rules to leave the king in check or to move it into check. There can be three ways to save the king.

1. Simply move the king out of the way of the rook's line of fire to any one of the squares marked with a cross.

2. Block the check by moving the bishop to stand in the rook's line of fire.

3. Easily the best, on this occasion, is to take the checking piece, by bishop takes rook.

Getting Out of Check

When your king is in check, it has to move out of check. Just watch . . .

The rook checks the black king.

The king moves out of check.

The black bishop gives check. Should White interpose the rook or move the king?

Kg1–h1 is the better idea. White would lose a rook for a bishop, equal to the loss of two pawns, if the rook were used to block the check.

Capturing the Checker

Below, the white pawn has given check. It is possible to capture it with either the black king or the black rook. But the king must not be put into check from the white rook. The king cannot take yet. However, the black rook can take the pawn.

Then, if White's rook captures Black's rook, the king can in turn take it. With only two kings remaining, and neither with a supporting army, the game is drawn.

CHECKMATE

If the king cannot escape from check, then he is checkmated. The word 'checkmate' comes from the Arabic 'shah mat' which means 'the king is dead'. The game is immediately over.

Black cannot take the checking white rook.

Nor has the king a neighbouring square off the rank to move to.
There is nothing available to interpose.
It is checkmate.

Sample Checkmates

The white queen checks the black king. The king's way off the back rank is blocked by the white king. It is checkmate.

The white rook checks the black king. The king's way off the back rank is blocked by the white king. Again, it is checkmate.

The white rook gives check along the back rank. The black king's way off this row is blocked by its own pawns. Once more, it is checkmate.

One of the white rooks gives check. This time the king's way off the rank is covered and prevented by the other white rook. Checkmate.

The King is Cornered

Black gives checkmate next move. Can you see how in each of these cases?

1.

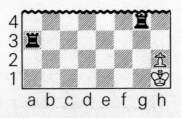

2.

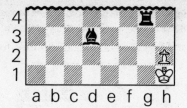

3.

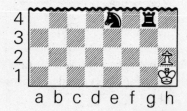

4.

Answers
1. ... Ra3–a1   2. ... Bd3–e4
3. ... Ne4–f2   4. ... Rc2–h2

36

Test Checkmates

Here is a test for you to do to learn to look for checkmating situations.

1. White to move. There are two different ways to check-mate the black king here.

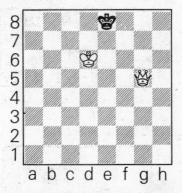

2. Black to move. Another back rank checkmate.

3. Black to move. The queen needs the bishop's protection to give checkmate.

4. Black to move. The queen and knight link up on to same square.

5. White to move. Another queen and knight act.

6. White to move. The bishop covers two of the black king's flight squares. The knight gives checkmate.

7. Black to move. The bishop hems in the white king. The rook finishes it.

8. White to move. One bishop cuts off the king's escape squares. The other gives checkmate.

9. Black to move. Again, one bishop prevents the king's escape, while the other gives checkmate.

10. Black to move. The knight helps the rook to give checkmate.

Answers

1. Qg5–e7 or Qg5–g8 2. Ra8–a1 3. Qd5–g2 4. Qc2–g2
5. Qd3–h7 6. Nf5–h6 7. Re8–g8 8. Bd3–a6 9. Bf5–e4
10. Rf8–f1

HOW CHESS BEAT THE GUILLOTINE: A TRUE STORY

It was summer in the year 1793 and the place was Paris. Monsieur Robespierre was striding along to his favourite café, the Café de la Régence. He was the Chairman of the Revolution, the boss of the Terror, and on his word the young aristocrats, the counts and countesses, went to their death at the guillotine. All the famous men of Paris came to this café and their chief relaxation was chess. Robespierre was a very good player.

Somewhere just outside of Paris a beautiful young girl was crying. Her name was Jacqueline Armand and her young fiancé, the Duc d'Eltine, had been sentenced to death. His crime was that he was a duke. Jacqueline was desperate to free her young man. She knew of Robespierre's liking for chess and that the Café was only for men. She cut off her shoulder-length hair and dressed as a young man of the Revolution, and went along to see if she could meet the man who controlled life and death for her young man.

Robespierre had just finished a game; he played all comers. As soon as the seat opposite him was free, Jacqueline slipped into it.

'And what are the stakes?' Robespierre was a gambler and every game had its price.

'On my part, a special request if I win. If you win, I have enough money to pay.'

Somehow Robespierre guessed the game was a matter of life and death and was determined to win. The game reached this position. Robespierre was White and Jacqueline Armand was Black.

Robespierre pushed his advanced pawn to the far rank and promoted it to a new, second queen, leaving Jacqueline to move! But she could give checkmate.

She played Bh4–f6 checkmate. Robespierre was in double check: from the bishop and from the queen. It was double check and checkmate.

Robespierre looked up. 'What is your request, young man?' His eyes noted her fine face, and he added, 'or should I say young woman?'

Quick as a flash came the answer, 'The life of my fiancé, the Duc d'Eltine.'

Robespierre pondered. 'You have been very brave; braver than I should have believed possible. Your fiancé is free.'

Did You Know?

The travelling chess set was invented by the Vikings. In their long ships, the Vikings packed chess sets in their sea-chests. The boards had little holes in them, and the chessmen had small pegs in their bases to fit the holes. They were made this way so that the boats pitching in a rough sea would not upset and ruin the game.

3. PREPARING FOR BATTLE

'The pawns are the soul of the game.'

André Philidor (1726–1795)

PUFFIN PAWNS

As a way of introducing the 'Lincolnshire Pawn Game', first published by the present authors and now used the world over, even in the USSR, we now present the 'Puffin Pawns'. The winner in these special games is the one who first gets a pawn to the other side of the board and replaces it with a queen.

Game 1. Black to move.

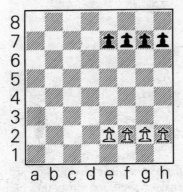

Game 2. White to move.

Game 3. Black to move.

Remember that pawns move directly forward one square at a time, except that, on their first move, they each can be moved either one or two squares ahead and they capture by moving one square diagonally forward and removing the enemy chessman.

PASSED PAWNS

Q. What is a passed pawn?

A. Late in the game, as pieces are exchanged, pawns can become very important: if one reaches the other end of the board, it will become a queen. That increases its value by eight pawns! (Remember: the queen equals nine pawns.) A pawn with a clear run through to the other side is called a passed pawn.

Here, Black's a-pawn is passed and is three squares away from becoming a queen.

A pawn can become a passed pawn by breaking through the enemy lines.

Black's a-pawn is not passed. But beware! Black to move can win.

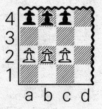

Black plays the centre pawn forward one square.

1 ...   b4–b3

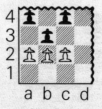

White takes with the a-pawn.

   2 a2 × b3

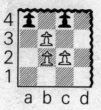

Now look carefully. White's pawn at b2 is guarding against the advance of Black's a4-pawn. How can Black get b2 out of the way? Black offers the c-pawn as bait!

   2 . . .   c4–c3

White has to take, otherwise the b-pawn itself will be captured on the next move, and Black will have a passed pawn. Therefore White plays

   3 b2 × c3

Now, the black pawn can march straight through.

3 ...   a4–a3

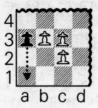

And a1 is reached in two more moves.

Here's another example:

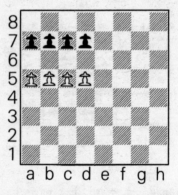

White begins. What can you make of this? Which pawn does White move first to clear a way through Black's rank?

Try **1 b5–b6**.

If Black replies with **1 ... a7 × b6**, then White responds with **2 c5–c6**. Black must then take the c-pawn, otherwise this can become a passed pawn. Black can capture in two ways. If Black replies with **2 ... b7 × c6**, then White can advance the a-pawn and it becomes a passed pawn. If, on the other hand, Black replies with **2 ... d7 × c6**, White responds with **3 d5 × c6**. Then Black must play **3 ... b7 × c6**, otherwise White's c-pawn can become

a passed pawn on the next move. Finally, White plays
4 a5–a6, and this is now a passed pawn.

After White's first move **1 b5–b6**, Black could have captured with **1 . . . c7 × b6**. Then, for White to gain a
passed pawn, the sequence of moves will be as follows:

    2 a5–a6   **b7 × a6**
    3 c5–c6   **d7 × c6**
    4 d5–d6 or d5 × c6

And White's pawn is now a passed pawn.

Set up the pawns again and try **1 c5–c6**. See if you can
break Black's rank. Play through all the possible moves with a
friend.

THE LINCOLNSHIRE PAWN GAME

The Lincolnshire line-up is eight pawns against eight pawns.

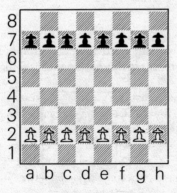

White, as usual, goes first. He or she whose pawn reaches the
far rank first is declared the winner. With care, and after
practice, you will end up with totally blocked positions. The
first to run out of moves loses.

QUEENING A PAWN

As mentioned earlier, when a pawn reaches the end of a file, that is, the opponent's back rank, it is promoted to a queen or any other chosen piece apart from a king. This is particularly useful at the end of games and can prove to be a game winner.

The dream position: from this position, White, with just a king and a pawn, can win the game by promoting the pawn to a queen. But reaching this position takes some skill.

Let us start from this position.

The white king at c5 is ready to shepherd his pawn through to glory. He advances to gain control of the square where his pawn will become a queen.

1 Kc5–c6   **1 . . . Kc8–b8**   **2 Kc6–d7**

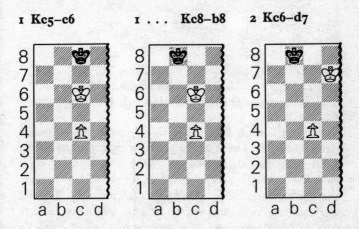

The white king now has control of the vital square. With **2 . . . Kb8–b7** and **3 c4–c5**, we have reached the dream position, from where the pawn can advance, and nothing can block its path, to c8 and promotion to a queen!

BISHOP TAKES ALL

Normally the white bishop (worth only three pawns) would stand no chance. But in this game all the enemy pieces kindly stand still and wait to be taken off! White is allowed only eight moves and there are eight chessmen for the bishop to take. You can't waste a move. Don't touch any piece yet. Try and work out in your mind's eye the order in which you need to take all the black pieces. Can you do it? Do you finish by taking the knight?

The solution:
Bf1 × c4 × e6 × c8 × b7 × f3 × h5 × f7 × g8.

ROOK TAKES ALL

This is a little bit harder, but still you might be able to do it without your chessboard. Remember the *white rook is the only piece that moves*. The rest stand like statues on a monument. Can you take all ten pieces in ten moves exactly?

One possible solution:
Re4 × c4 × c6 × e6 × h6 × h7 × e7 × e3 × b3 × b5 × h5.

THE KNIGHT'S DRIVING TEST

You have eighteen moves to take all the black pawns, which remain fixed.

First take the h7 pawn, and then the remaining pawns ringed in the diagram, to reach b7.

You will then find yourself in this position. Now, do a three-point turn to take a7 followed by the remaining pawns.

Complete the three-point turn via d8 and c6, or d6 and c8, or d6 and b5, or even a5 and c6. Going via c5 takes at least five moves.

One solution to the 'knight's driving test' is given below. First make for the h7 pawn:

1 Ng1–f3   2 Nf3–g5   3 Ng5 × h7

then capture the ringed pawns:

4 Nh7–g5   7 Ne5 × d7
5 Ng5 × f7   8 Nd7–c5
6 Nf7–e5   9 Nc5 × b7

and now the three-point turn:

10 Nb7–a5   11 Na5–c6   12 Nc6 × a7

and then the home run:

13 Na7–b5   16 Nd5 × e7
14 Nb5 × c7   17 Ne7–f5
15 Nc7–d5   18 Nf5 × g7

If you practise this often, you will learn to journey with the knight all over the board, and, like former World Champion Karpov, see the best squares and routes for it.

THE KINGS' DUEL

The winner of this royal duel will be the first king to reach the other side of the board. Although it is customary for White to move first, in this game try Black, who should win.

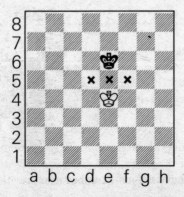

58

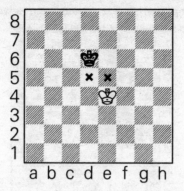

Remember! Kings cannot move on to squares that are next to each other. That would be the same as moving into check. For example, neither king can move on to the squares labelled with a cross in the above diagrams.

KING AND PAWNS VERSUS KING AND PAWNS

The king and pawn duel. First pawn to the other side wins.

White to start as is customary. Game plan: advance the king quickly and get him among the enemy pawns.

No go area! Remember the king cannot move into check on any of the squares labelled with a cross.

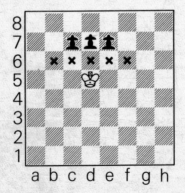

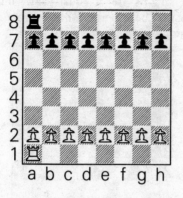

Win by being the first one to take all the enemy pawns. Game plan: use your rooks to mop up the enemy pawns. Play with a friend, making one move each in turn. Remember that when a rook captures an enemy pawn, the pawn is removed from the board and the rook takes its place. Beware of the pawn's diagonal capture!

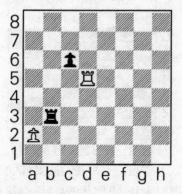

Here, both rooks can be taken: the white rook by the pawn on c6, and the black rook by the pawn on a2.

BISHOP AND PAWNS VERSUS KNIGHT AND PAWNS

First, let us see which is better: the bishop or the knight? Bishops and knights are of equal value, but, in a given situation, one may be preferable to the other. Let us look at a couple of examples.

Here, the white bishop can act on both wings. It can hold up the advance of either pawn. There is no place from where a knight could do the same.

However, in this situation, the black knight can jump in amongst the pawns. It can be brought to d4 to attack White's b3-pawn, while the bishop can attack nothing and is tied to defending.

To sum up, the bishop has the ability to attack at long range, while the knight has excellent manoeuvrability in crowded situations.

Now to the game:

The first pawn through to the other side wins. Play with a friend, taking it in turns to have the bishop and the knight, and see which you prefer.

Did You Know?

Bobby Fischer, born in 1943, champion of the USA when he was only fourteen, became the youngest ever Grandmaster at fifteen. In 1972, Fischer beat the Soviet Boris Spassky to become the only non-Soviet World Champion since 1946. Gary Kasparov, born in Baku in Soviet Central Asia, became the World Champion at the age of twenty-two in 1985.

4. LET BATTLE BEGIN

'Help your pieces so that they can help you.'

Paul Morphy (1837–1884)

DRAWING UP THE BATTLE LINES

At the beginning of a game, the chessmen are always arranged in the same regular formation on the board. Remember that the chessboard is positioned so that each player has a light square in their nearest right-hand corner. The chessmen can then be set up as follows.

First, the rooks, stately and castle-like, are set in the corners.

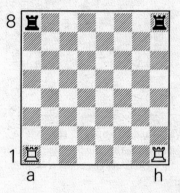

Then the four knights ride out to the squares next to the rooks.

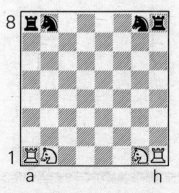

Then the lordly bishops, ready for the fray on their diagonals, take their places alongside the knights.

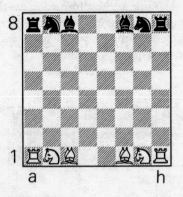

Then the rival queens appear: the white queen goes to the white square and the black queen to her usual black square. They face each other across the board, ready for the imminent battle.

Finally come the kings, who take their ceremonial places beside the queens. Their foot-soldiers, the pawns, line the next rank. All is ready.

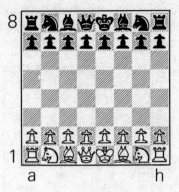

A DREAM START

A good way to begin your game is by moving out your centre pawns. This allows your bishops and queen to come into play.

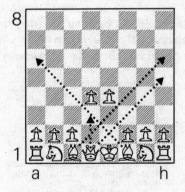

Next, bring out the knights and bishops. They should be ready to attack from and through the centre part of the board: the squares within the area c3–c6–f6–f3. Also, take the opportunity to move your queen into this area so that she can be used to help mount an attack. But always take care when moving your queen: she is your most valuable piece!

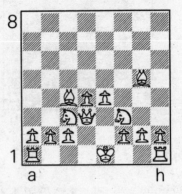

Then your king can be tucked safely away behind guarding pawns. This is achieved by a manoeuvre called castling, which is explained below. Castling also frees the rooks so that they can be placed on the partly open d- and e-files, ready for a door to be opened into the heart of the enemy position.

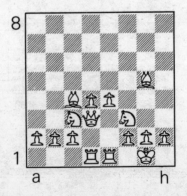

How many moves did that take? Two for the pawns, two for the knights, two for the bishops, one for the queen, one to castle and two for the rooks, making a total of ten moves. But, at every move, please remember to look at what your opponent is trying to do. You hope to make your dream start, but you will be wide awake and ready to respond to your opponent.

SPECIAL MOVES

Castling

Castling is a special move for the king and rook. It is the only time when the king can move two squares and when a rook jumps over a piece. This special move came about because players used to spend a long time getting their kings tucked in behind the pawns for protection. Castling makes this easy for both players.

In order to castle, we move the king two squares towards the rook and then we move the rook over the king on to the square alongside. Castling constitutes one move. It can be done with either of the rooks, and so we talk of 'castling on the king's side' and 'castling on the queen's side'.

Before castling

After castling

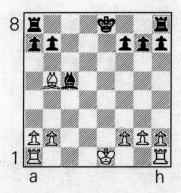

Rules of castling

1. It must be both the king's and the rook's first move of the game.
2. There must be no pieces between the king and the rook.
3. You cannot castle while you are in check or if the king has to cross a square on which he would be in check.

A castling quiz

Can Black, on his or her next move, castle in the following positions?

1

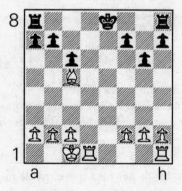

Answers

1. The king cannot castle at the moment. He is in check from the white bishop.
2. The king cannot castle towards the a-rook, because he will land in check on c8. He can castle to g8, with the h-rook coming to f8.
3. The black king cannot castle to c8 while the square d8 is under attack from the white rook. Similarly, he cannot castle to g8 while the white bishop attacks f8.
4. The king can castle either side to c8 or g8. It does not matter that one black rook is under attack from a white bishop and the other rook must cross the square b8 which is under attack from the same white bishop.

Special Pawn Capture

When a pawn is moved two squares forward on its first move, it can be taken by an enemy pawn, on the very next move only, as though it had only moved one square. This move is called 'en passant' (say 'on passon'), which is French for 'in passing'.

You are White. The black pawn on c7 advances two squares from c7 to c5.

It must be your very next move. You push the black pawn back one square to c6, and then you can take it: all in one move.

And it's all part of the same special move: *en passant*.

Now try the Lincolnshire Pawn Game (see p. 51) using this special *en passant* move.

ENDING THE FIGHT QUICKLY

Fool's Checkmate

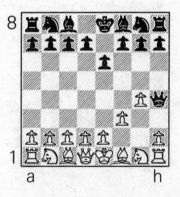

It is only Black's second move and it is checkmate. The king cannot move off the diagonal of the black queen. White's pieces can neither block the black queen, nor take the queen. It is checkmate! The sequence of moves was as follows:

1 f2–f3   e7–e6
2 g2–g4   Qd8–h4   **checkmate.**

This game between two very strong players took place in
1925. The moves went as follows:

    1 d2–d4   Ng8–f6
    2 Nb1–d2   e7–e5
    3 d4 × e5

This attacks the black knight.

    3 · · ·   Nf6–g4

The knight is now ready to take back the pawn on e5.

4 h2–h3 (Not a useful move: no piece comes into play. Indeed White's move leads to disaster.)

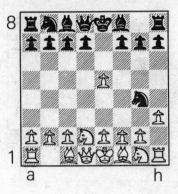

4 ... Ng4–e3 (Attacking White's queen. Where can he go? Nowhere.)

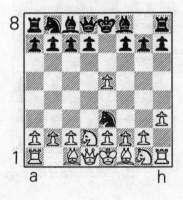

5 f2 × e3 (No choice: he had to take the attacker. But now Black can check.)

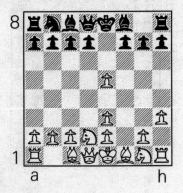

5 . . . Qd8–h4 check.

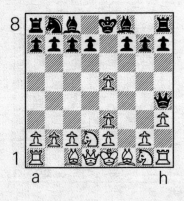

6 g2–g3 (The only move that will block check.)

6 ... Qh4 × g3 checkmate.

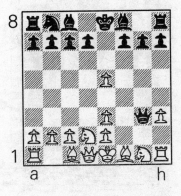

THE MERCHANT AND THE ARAB

A Spanish merchant was travelling round Spain doing business in all the big towns. One day, while riding on a lonely road, he came across an Arab sitting in the middle of the road playing chess by himself.

The merchant was curious and asked, 'Why are you playing chess all by yourself in the middle of the road?'

'I am not alone,' said the Arab.

'But I can't see anyone with you?'

'Ah,' replied the Arab, 'that is because I am playing the great Allah, the one who is everywhere!'

'You have a powerful opponent then!'

'Yes, but he is a fair one.'

'And is he winning?' asked the merchant.

'I think so. Can you see how I can avoid being checkmated by His next move? It will mean that I can't play any more today!'

'Why not?'

'I've lost all my money,' replied the Arab.

'Do you and Allah always play chess for money?'

'Yes. This game will cost me twenty gold pieces.'

'But how will you pay Allah the money?' inquired the merchant, who had never heard of anyone gambling on a game of chess with Allah before.

'Oh, that is easy. Of course, Allah doesn't take the money himself, but He sends some honest, holy man who will take it and give it to the poor. That is the same as giving it to Allah. You must be the man whom Allah has sent today. So here, do Allah's bidding and take these twenty gold pieces.'

The merchant, who wasn't as honest as he should have been, was delighted. He couldn't wait until the next time he travelled on that road to find out if Allah was still winning his games with the Arab. As it happened it was a few weeks before he was on that road again. But there was the same Arab, sitting over a chess game as before.

'Is Allah winning today?' asked the merchant.

'No,' replied the Arab. 'In one more move I shall checkmate Him!'

'And how much money will you win?'

'One hundred gold pieces!'

'But how will Allah pay you?' asked the merchant in surprise.

'Oh, that is easy. Of course, Allah doesn't pay me himself, but He sends some honest, holy man who will give me what I have won. You must be the man whom Allah has sent today to pay me the hundred gold pieces.'

5. SKILLS

'Do not regard your opponent as a sheep, but rather as a wolf.'

Russian Proverb

THE FORK

A fork occurs when one piece attacks two or more enemy pieces at the same time. All the chess pieces are capable of forking, even the humble pawn. Let us look at the pawn fork.

The white pawn will move forward to fork the knight and rook. One of them will be taken on the next move because Black cannot capture the pawn, nor can he or she move both the knight and the rook in one move.

But the most frightening fork of all is the knight fork. In the position shown here, the white knight attacks the king and queen simultaneously (a royal fork). Black must now get out of check, leaving the queen to be captured on the next move.

Can you see how the knight can fork in the following cases? First, we have two examples of the royal fork. The white knight moves to attack the enemy king and queen at the same time in both diagrams.

Answer: Ne7–c6

Answer: Ng5–e6

Now the black knight moves to fork the queen and the rook. Can you see how in each case?

Answer: Nb4–d3

Answer: Nf1–e3

A Devastating Fork

Don't bring your queen out too early. The queen is the strongest piece on the board and, after the king, she is easily the most valuable. Be careful about bringing her into battle too soon. She may herself become a target for an attack. Let's see what happens in this game.

1 e2–e4   e7–e5
This is a common way for chess games to begin.

2 Bf1–c4   Qd8–g5

Black's strongest piece enters the battle alone and she becomes a target for the attention of the white pieces.

3 Ng1–f3

First, the knight comes out to attack. The queen eyes the pawn on g2 greedily.

3 · · ·   Qg5 × g2

Rather than retreat, the queen grabs the white pawn. Now the white rook comes out of the corner to attack her.

4 Rh1–g1

The white rook is protected by its knight. White has now brought three pieces into the affray: the bishop, the knight and the rook. The black queen has only one safe move.

4 . . .   Qg2–h3

White could take the pawn on e5 with the knight. But there is also a chance to attack the black queen. White sizes the pawn on f7 with the bishop and gives check to the black king. What is the plan?

5 Bc4 × f7 check

Black moves immediately and captures the bishop on f7.

5 . . . Ke8 × f7

Black did not see the danger. Did you? White's knight can now give check, forking Black's king and queen.

6 Nf3–g5 check

A royal fork. After the king moves out of check, the white knight will take the black queen. It came out dangerously early and it has been lost.

PINNING

'The pin is mightier than the sword.'

Fred Reinfeld

If you attack an enemy piece which guards the way to a more valuable one, you *pin* it. Thus, your opponent can't move that piece without exposing him or herself to a more serious attack.

In the diagrams below, the white bishop moves to f3, attacking the rook. If the rook moves, White will be able to take the queen. The black rook is said to be pinned against the queen.

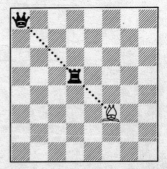

In this position, the rook can be pinned against the king by the white bishop. Can you see how? When thus pinned, the rook cannot be moved, since this would put the king in check.

Answer: Be2–c4

And can you see how the black rook can pin the white knight against its king?

Answer: Ra1–a4

White plays Be2–f3 to pin the black rook at d5. Black hits back with Rc8–f8, pinning the white bishop against its king. Finally, White pins the black rook at f8 against its king by Rg1–g8.

Here is a really lovely demonstration of the power of the pin to achieve a checkmate.

It is White's move. The white rook attacks the black king.

1 Rc8–h8 check

Black must take.

1 ...   Kh7 × h8

The black pawn on g7 must stay to protect the black king from White's bishop at b2. It is pinned to the h2–h8 diagonal. Now can you see where the white queen can swoop?

2 Qc1–h6 check

The pinned pawn cannot take it. The black king must move.

2 . . .   Kh8–g8

And now the white queen gives checkmate, using that remote bishop for support, by **3 Qh6 × g7**.

It is the end of the game. The king cannot be moved because of the white queen, and the queen cannot be taken because of the bishop.

THE SKEWER

A skewer is a situation in which a valuable piece is attacked and forced to move, leaving another (unprotected) piece to be taken.

Here is a rook skewer:

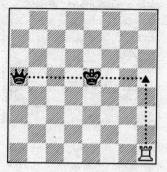

The white rook moves to skewer the black king and queen. It gives check. The king must move out of check and this leaves the queen to be taken.

Here is a skewer by a bishop:

Again, the king is in check, and therefore must move, leaving the white queen at the bishop's mercy.

DISCOVERED ATTACK

Discovered attack is a particularly effective attacking move. It occurs when a player moves a piece which then allows another of his or her pieces to attack an enemy piece. Here is an example.

When the black rook moves, it uncovers the black bishop, which gives check.

Now, this leads to interesting possibilities. How much more dastardly it would be if the rook could move to attack or take something valuable and still leave the king to get out of check!

Can you see the best square to which to move the rook? Rg2–a2 to attack the queen is right! Black must now move the king out of check, leaving the white rook to take the queen on the following move.

Nunn Plays Discovered Attack

John Nunn is one of Britain's strongest players. In this game, played at the 1986 Chess Olympiad in Dubai, he is Black against Zapata of Columbia. It is John's turn to move. Do you see how he can discover an attack against the white queen and win it?

Nunn (Black)

Zapata (White)

The black knight seems to be pinned: if it is moved, White can play Qd1 × g4 to take Black's queen. However, the black knight can be moved in such a way that White has no time to take Black's queen. How?

1 . . .   Ne2–g3 check

White must now get out of check, giving Black the time to take the white queen.

Kasparov Plays Skewer and Discovered Attack

Gary Kasparov became World Champion at the age of twenty-two. It is not often that we see a skewer and a discovered attack in the space of a few moves, but Kasparov (White) has the possibility to play both in this game, which came up at the 1986 Chess Olympiad in Dubai. First, the skewer:

Tatai (Black)

Kasparov (White)

White's queen at g7 has Black's king in check. Notice that the black king could take the white knight. But if it does . . .

Do you see how White can play a skewer in this position?

Qg7–f8 check

Black's king must now move out of check off the diagonal, allowing the white queen to take the black queen at the far end of the diagonal.

Tatai saw this, so instead he played . . .

1 . . .   Ke7–d8

Kasparov responded with . . .

2 Qg7–f8 check

At the same time, he was looking through the white knight towards the black queen, thus providing an opportunity for discovered attack. Black has two replies: he can move the bishop to e8 to block the check or he can move the king to c7. What should he do?

If 2 . . . Bd7–e8, White replies with 3 Q × B check, the white queen being protected by the knight. This drives the black king to c7, whereupon White plays 4 Nd6–b5 to produce a royal fork with the knight.

If Black's king moves immediately to c7, then White un-covers his queen to attack the black queen by moving his knight with check either by Nd6–e8 or by Nd6–b5.

So, either way, the black queen is captured and the game is lost.

DRAWN GAMES

There are a number of ways in which a game can result in a draw.

Agreement

You can have a draw by agreeing such with your opponent. Two players are likely to agree on a draw when they decide that they do not have enough of their armies left to give checkmate. This occurs, for example, when there are only two kings remaining on the board. Also, it is impossible to checkmate with a king and a single bishop or a king and one knight only. It would therefore be a waste of time to continue playing in such a position.

Stalemate

The game is drawn if either you or your opponent is stalemated. For this to happen to you, three conditions must be satisfied:

(i)   it must be your move;
(ii) you must not be in check;
(iii) you cannot make *any* moves according to the rules.

These conditions can equally apply to your opponent, in which case he or she is stalemated, and the game is drawn.

Here is a stalemate. It is White's move, but the white king (which is not in check) cannot move without going into check.

Perpetual Check or Repeated Positions

When it is perpetual check, or indeed if the same position keeps on being repeated, a draw can be claimed after it has happened three times. Here is an example.

The Fifty Move Rule

If nothing changes – that is, no pawns have moved and there have been no captures – for fifty moves on each side, a draw can be claimed. So, when you are left with a king and a rook or a king and a queen, or other similar combinations of pieces, against a lone king, you must give checkmate in fifty of your moves.

In this position, the black king and queen must give checkmate in less than fifty moves. With practice, this can be done in less than twelve moves.

Sample Stalemates

Here are some sample stalemates, with White to try and move. Remember, stalemate is a draw, not a win.

If you have a queen more than your opponent and you fail to win, you feel worse than if you had lost the game!

In the positions below, work out how White can move and avoid putting Black in stalemate.

1

2

3

Answers

1. *Not* Kd5–c5 nor Kd5–c6.
2. *Not* Kd6–c7 immediately; recommend instead first Qc6–b5, then Kd6–c7.
3. *Not* Qd6–c7; recommend either Qd6–d7 or Ke5–d5.

If you choose the wrong move, you fail to win – you give stalemate.

CHECKMATE!

The Four Move Checkmate and How to Prevent It

The opening moves have been as follows:

  1 e2–e4   e7–e5
  2 Qd1–h5   Nb8–c6

Black brings out the knight and defends the pawn on e5. Good move.

3 Bf1–c4

Now, as the player of the white pieces knows, both the white bishop and queen are converging on Black's pawn at f7: two pieces attacking it, with only the black king defending. Red alert! Red alert!

3 ... Ng8–f6

Black fails to notice. His alarm bells do not ring. He's intent on attacking the white queen. Now the queen and bishop stand ready for the kill. It's the end.

4 Qh5 × f7 check

How can the black king get out of check? He cannot take the white queen: she is protected by her bishop. Nothing else can take the white queen. Can the black king move out of check? The only available square is e7, and this is covered by the white queen also. The king is lost – it is checkmate!

Let us now see how we can prevent the four move checkmate.

Again, the white queen and bishop are lined up against the weak pawn on f7. How do we meet the threat? By bringing in extra protection with Qd8–e7, Qd8–f6 or Ng8–h6? Or by putting something in the way with g7–g6? Black chooses this last option.

3 · · ·   g7–g6

The white queen retreats.

4 Qh5–f3

Now there's a threat to move the queen up the f-file and take the pawn on f7, once again giving checkmate. Be vigilant! Both the queen and the bishop still attack the pawn on f7. Black blocks the way with . . .

That's another piece in play. White responds with . . .

5 g2–g4

White intends to play this pawn one square further forward on the next move, hoping to force the knight away. White is still trying to break through to checkmate at f7. Black now begins a counter-attack.

5 ...   Nc6–d4

This attacks the white queen, but it also attacks the pawn at c2.

6 Qf3–e3

This is a really short-sighted move. It doesn't protect c2, and, after Black takes the pawn on c2, it will be check. But not only that! It is a family fork: the white king, queen and rook will all be attacked by the black knight.

6 ... Nd4 × c2 check

After the king moves out of check, the black knight can take either the queen or the rook – not a difficult choice!

The four move checkmate has been stopped and, indeed, Black has gained the advantage. Black is a piece to the good and takes the initiative from White.

Checkmate with the King and Queen

The checkmate with the king and powerful queen against the king is one of the easiest to learn. This checkmate happens often, because in many, many games the winning plan is to push a pawn through to become a queen. Thus, knowing how to give this most common of checkmates is very important.

How terrible it is to get a new queen and not know how to finish the game. It's like having the ball at your feet in football, an open goalmouth in front of you, no defender nearby, and then kicking the ball high over the bar.

Sample Checkmates

Checkmate along the rank or file:

Checkmate with the queen protected by its king:

Notice that, in each case, the king which is checkmated is on the edge of the board and the other king plays a necessary and essential role in the checkmate.

Handy Tips

Here are three tips to help you improve your technique in handling this ending:

1. Drive the king to be checkmated to an edge of the board.
2. To help close the net, bring your king nearer your opponent's king at every opportunity, because it is slower moving than the queen.
3. There is little need to give check *en route*.

Sample Endgame

We have the black king and queen versus the lone white king.

1 ...   Kb1–c2

2 Ke6–d5

The lone king tries to stay in the centre.

2 ...   Kc2–d3

Black moves nearer with the king.

3 Kd5–c5   Qa1–f6

One can't bring the black king much closer. Hence, the queen moves to cut the lone king off from ranks 6, 7 and 8.

4 Kc5–d5

Black still cannot bring the king closer, so plays . . .

4 · · ·   Qf6–e7

This limits the escape of the white king to one square.

5 Kd5–c6

Now Black moves nearer with the pursuing king.

5 ...   Kd3–c4

Again, the white king can only go to one square.

6 Kc6–b6

Now, the black king cannot approach next to the white one, so . . .

6 . . .   Qe7–d7

And the white king must go on to the fatal squares on the edge of the board.

7 Kb6–a6

The moment that the defending king reaches the edge can be critical. *Watch for stalemate*. Stalemate gives you only a draw; you want to win. *Do not play* 7 . . . Qd7–c7.

7 . . .   Kc4–c5

The white king has only one move:
8 Ka6–a5
Now Black has a choice of mates:
8 . . .   Qd7–a7
or
8 . . .   Qd7–b5
That took eight moves. Good team work!

Checkmate with the Knight

The nimble knight can give checkmate. We will show you one and then leave you to do the puzzles below.

The knight lands on f7 and gives check over the top of the black pieces surrounding their king. The king cannot move. He is smothered, boxed in, by his own pieces. It's checkmate.

Six Puzzles

In each puzzle, it is the white knight to move and give checkmate. What is the move?

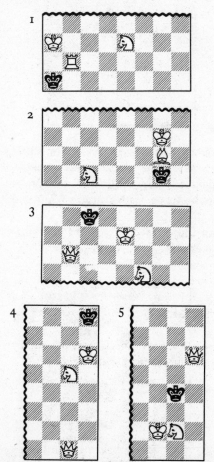

6

Answers

1. Ne3–c2. 2. Nc1–e2. 3. Nf5–d6.
4. Ng5–f7. 5. Ng2–e3. 6. Nd4–b3.

Capablanca Plays a Knight Checkmate

It is very difficult to calculate many moves. Checks to a king
or attack by checkmating threats make it easier. Here is a
series of forcing moves by the legendary Capablanca, World
Champion in the 1920s. Capablanca is White and it is Black
to move.

Capablanca threatens both Ng5–f7 checkmate and also
Qh4 × h7 checkmate.

1 . . .   Qd6–g6

This stops the white knight moving: it is now pinned along the g-file against the white king. Despite this, White gives checkmate in two moves.

2 Qh4 × h7 check

There is only one reply to this move. The king cannot take, as it would then be in check from the knight.

2 . . .   Qg6 × h7

White has given up – we say sacrificed – his queen. Now, can you see the checkmate? Have you noticed that the white knight has suddenly become free to move again?

3 Ng5–f7 checkmate.

The black king is boxed in.

Did You Know?

An endgame problem set by Al-Adli in an Arab manuscript of the ninth century came up in actual play in 1945 in a game in Denmark.

---

6. GREAT CHESS

'He was the greatest player that ever lived.'

Fischer on Morphy

PAUL MORPHY: 'THE PRIDE AND SORROW OF CHESS'

When He Was Young

It was a beautiful house in New Orleans: a judge's house. The logs in the fireplace were still glowing. Two brothers were finishing a game of chess. Watching was Alonzo's eight-year-old son, Paul. The two men took no notice of him. He knew the names of the pieces, but that was all.

The game was over and Uncle Ernest out in the street when Paul turned to his father and said, 'You made a mistake in that game, father: you could have won.'

Alonzo Morphy was packing away the pieces into their box. He was only half-listening; anyway he could not remember the position. The boy could. Quickly, he reconstructed the position where his father had made the final mistake. Alonzo looked long and hard, completely astonished. His wife was still awake when he went to bed.

'Did you know,' he asked her, 'that we have another chess player in the family?'

Paul Morphy was to become one of the greatest players of all time.

Morphy's Brilliant Finish: Checkmate with Rook and Bishop

In 1858, when he was only twenty-one years old, Morphy toured Europe playing, and beating, all the best chess players. By this time he was a celebrity and his company was sought by all the aristocrats of Europe. In Paris he often dined with the Duke of Brunswick and was a frequent guest in the Duke's box at the opera house. The Duke, a keen chess player himself, kept a set of chessmen and board in his box at the opera house. One evening, during a performance of the *Barber of Seville*, the Duke, together with the Count of Isouard, challenged Morphy to a game of chess. In order that he should better concentrate, Morphy was made to play with his back to the stage. But Morphy was fond of opera, and contrived this remarkable finish so that he could watch the performance.

This is the position after fifteen moves. Morphy is White and it is his move.

16 Qb3–b8 check

Black is in check. The black knight must take the queen.

Of course, Morphy does not give away queens for nothing. Can you see why he wanted the black knight moved? Can you see the checkmate?

16 ... Nd7 × b8

Now Morphy could turn around and watch the opera!

17 Rd1–d8 checkmate

Here is another rook and bishop checkmate. This game, played in 1911, has a similar finish to Morphy's. Can you see it?

Alapin (Black)

Nimzowitsch (White)

Just like Morphy, Nimzowitsch is ready for the final blow. He would like to shift the bishop at e7. Why? Because it is in the way of his e1-rook.

1 Qd2–d8 check   Be7 × d8

Now for the checkmate:

2 Re1–e8 checkmate.

WHEN KINGS WERE KINGS

Queen Galienne was dressed all in white silk, plain and simple, among all the gold thread and displays of ermine of the court. Yet she moved among the crowds with poise. She was Charlemagne's queen.

Charlemagne's court was busy today. Cupbearers were bustling to the great tables, carrying huge pitchers of wine. Trains of servants came carrying silver platters of hot meats. As Galienne picked her way through the crowd, her eyes strayed to the non-stop theatre where jugglers were manipulating gleaming razor-sharp daggers, acrobats were perched precariously on poles and Saracen girls were balancing on fast-spinning balls. Galienne was off to see the tournament.

Garin was fighting today. Galienne liked him and she

enjoyed tournaments with the huge, heavy French horses, barrel-bodied and thundering the ground with their hooves. She liked the splintering lances and the ladies throwing glances at the knights. She was there to receive the tournament winner. She hoped it would be Garin.

Six marshals led by Roland, Charlemagne's favourite noble, led the knights out. Trumpets sounded and Roland shouted, 'Let the joust begin! In the name of God and St Michael do battle.' When Garin and his opponent appeared, a huge roar went up. It was easy to be excited.

Garin was everybody's favourite and ribbons from the ladies fluttered down. As the crowds expected, so it turned out to be. Garin unseated his opponent with the first blow of his lance. Garin defeated knight after knight after knight until it was certain that he had won the tournament.

Galienne moved away from the tournament stands to the reception tent where she would receive the winner. Her heart beat fast and her thoughts raced as Garin knelt before her to receive the tournament's first prize. Did Garin play chess? Would he agree to come and play her?

And so Garin agreed to Galienne's request. Garin liked Galienne too, but he was astonished when she told him she loved him. This was too much! After all, she was Charlemagne's queen and Charlemagne did not like people who got in his way. Hadn't he beheaded three thousand Saxons in one day because they would not be Christians? He was Emperor of all Europe. No! Garin could not return Galienne's love.

Queen Galienne was stunned. How dare this knight reject her? She would have her revenge and she didn't care how she got it. She told Charlemagne the whole story. Amazingly, Charlemagne agreed with her. A knight could not insult a queen. He spun on his heels and left the room. 'I will punish this insolent knight,' was his parting shot.

The next morning Charlemagne summoned Garin to his quarters and challenged him to a duel at chess. If Garin won, he would have the queen for his wife and the kingdom as well.

If Charlemagne won he would have Garin's head.

The game was fixed for the following morning. The two men sat down at the chessboard which had been given to Charlemagne by the Caliph of Baghdad, the world-famous Haroun al-Rashid. Garin knew his position to be desperate. There was no way, even if he won, that he could take Charlemagne's crown. And if he lost . . . the thought was terrible!

The game went as follows. (We give a modern version of what could have happened in the game. In Charlemagne's times, pawns only moved one square, the queen only one square and the bishop only two squares. But the legend is referred to by many chess historians.)

1 e2–e4   e7–e5

Both Charlemagne, who is White, and Garin move forward their centre pawns.

2 Ng1–f3   Ng8–f6

Both players then bring out their knights.

3 Nf3 × e5   Nb8–c6

Charlemagne plays to go a pawn ahead. Garin brings his pieces out quickly.

4 Ne5 × c6   d7 × c6

Both Black's bishops are now ready for play.

5 d2–d3   Bf8–c5

Charlemagne protects his pawn, but look! Garin has two pieces out; Charlemagne has none.

6 Bc1–g5   Nf6 × e4

At last Charlemagne has got a piece into play and Garin is going to lose his queen.

7 Bg5 × d8   Bc5 × f2 check

Yes, he has, but now comes a check to which White has only one reply.

White's only move.

8 ...   Bc8–g4 checkmate

And now Garin brings his bishop out to give check and checkmate.

Garin looked the king in the face. 'Let us forget those stakes, sire,' he said. Charlemagne suddenly smiled, a big, broad smile, dissolving all the tension. 'I love a sportsman and you certainly are one. From now on, you will be known as Garin of Montglane, Baron. Come let us be friends.' And so Charlemagne and Garin became firm friends, but it had been a very close call.

ALEKHINE'S DREAM

This story was told by Alexander Alekhine, World Champion 1927–1935 and 1937–1946.

'Last night,' he said, 'I dreamed that I had died. As I neared the gates of Heaven, I saw St Peter.

'"Who are you?" he asked me.

'"I am Alekhine. Don't you know? Chess champion of the world."

'"Sorry," said St Peter, shaking his head sadly. "There is no room in heaven for chess players." I was really upset, but before leaving I took one last look around. And who did I see? Why, none other than my portly friend Bogolyubov. Quickly, I pointed him out to St Peter.

'"Look, there's Bogolyubov," I said triumphantly. "He's a chess player! And he's in heaven."

'"No, you are wrong," St Peter replied quickly. "He only thinks he's a chess player."'

Did You Know?

The folding chessboard was invented by a priest! There used to be times when the church disliked chess very much. In A.D. 1125, Bishop Guy of Paris excommunicated all priests who played chess. One priest made a chessboard that looked like two books lying together. His idea became so popular that you'll still see many chessboards made in this way.

A CHESS GLOSSARY

Castling   A special move for the king and rook. The king moves two squares and the rook jumps over the king and stands alongside (pp. 70–73).

Check   When the king is attacked by an enemy piece.

Checkmate   When the king cannot escape from attack.

Diagonal   A line of squares going diagonally across the board: e.g. the white diagonal from h1–a8 which shows us the correct way to place the chessboard.

Double check   A position in which a king is in check from two pieces at once.

En passant   A special pawn move: see page 73.

File   A line of squares going up and down the board.

Fork   An attack by one piece on two enemy pieces at the same time.

J'adoube   The rule in chess is 'touch a piece, move it'. If you are going to touch a piece only to straighten it on its square, you should say 'j'adoube' or 'I adjust'. Otherwise, you could be required to move it.

Pin   Pieces are said to be 'pinned' when they cannot move without endangering another, more valuable, piece.

Passed pawn   This is a pawn which has a clear path – not obstructed by enemy pawns – to a queening square at the far rank of the board. Organize support for its rapid advance.

Open file   An open file is one on which there are no pawns. Rooks love open files; double them up on an open file to penetrate to the heart of the enemy.

Rank   A line of squares going from left to right or right to left across the board.

Skewer   An attack on an important piece which forces it to move, leaving another piece behind it to be taken.

Stalemate   This occurs when one player, although not in check, can make no legal move. Stalemate is not a win. It's a draw.

The book is ended and so is the game.
But I have gained a pleasing fame.
I found my thinking much improved
Because I learnt a certain move.
My queen was cornered
My king was checked
I was trapped and began to fret
But I used my skill and planned a scheme
Turning Rose's face quite green.
I beat Mary, lost to Sally
and found a pleasant friend in Harry!

INDEX

THE PUFFIN BOOK OF HANDWRITING
Tom Gourdie

How to write well with everyday materials. Write an alphabet in a tree of hearts, fill in word puzzles, trace letters, draw line patterns, have fun and acquire an elegant style of handwriting. These exercises have been devised to help you learn how to write beautifully.

THE PUFFIN BOOK OF DANCE
Craig Dodd

From ballet to Broadway, this book is packed with fascinating information for all young dance fans. From the evolution of dance in all its forms to dance classes, schools and techniques, the life of professional dancers, how dances are made and much more besides, this book captures the glamour and excitement of this spectacular art form.

PETS FOR KEEPS
Dick King-Smith

Keeping a pet can be fascinating and great fun, but it is important to choose the right pet: one that will fit in with your family and surroundings, one that you can afford to keep. This book is packed with useful information about budgies, hamsters, cats, guinea-pigs, mice, rabbits, gerbils, canaries, bantams, rats, goldfish and dogs – Dick King-Smith's expert advice and amusing stories about some of the pets he has known and loved make this a practical and entertaining book.

BET YOU CAN'T!
Vicki Cobb and Kathy Darling

Bet you can't resist trying out some of these tempting tricks on your family and friends. And you'll win the bet every time with such scientific impossibilities. For despite looking dead easy, the basic principles of gravity, mechanics, maths, perception, liquids and energy ensure that they cannot actually be performed!

CREEPY-CRAWLIES
Paul Temple

At last! All you could ever want to know about creepy-crawlies – spiders, worms, caterpillars, centipedes, tadpoles and many more extraordinary creatures. This amusing book is full of amazing facts and fun things to do – build a wormery, create a beehive, spy on pond creepy-crawlies with an underwater scope.

THE PUFFIN BOOK OF BRAINTEASERS
Eric Emmet

Hours of fun await you if you can tackle problems in this treasure chest of puzzles. Some are simple, some are (almost) impossible, but all are Brainteasers.